S0-AGX-533

Presented to: _____

From: _____

On the Occasion of: _____

_____

The Beauty of Love

LLOYD JOHN OGILVIE

The Beauty of Love

A Harvest House Special Edition

HARVEST HOUSE PUBLISHERS
Eugene, Oregon 97402

The Beauty of Love

Copyright © 1980 by Harvest House Publishers
Eugene, Oregon 97402

Library of Congress Catalog Card Number 80-80465
ISBN 0-89081-245-4

Printed in the United States of America.

Design by Koechel/Peterson Design
Minneapolis, Minnesota 55406

The Gift and the Giver

"The love that we need is God Himself coming into our hearts. When the soul is perfected in love, it has such a source of that love that it can rest in it for eternity, and though it has as much as it can contain for the time being, it can always receive more." Andrew Murray

God does not give love. He is love. When we receive Him, we experience love. It is impossible to separate the gift and the giver. God *is* unchanging, unqualified love. He wills the ultimate good of each of us. His love is not dependent upon our performance or even upon our response of loving Him. How do we know He loves us? He has told us through Jesus Christ, love incarnate. Christ is love in action—searching, pursuing, accepting, forgiving and cherishing you and me.

"That Christ may dwell in your hearts through faith; and you, being rooted and grounded in love, may be able to comprehend...the breadth and length and height and depth, and to know the love of Christ which surpasses knowledge, that you may be filled up to all the fullness of God."

Ephesians 3:17-19, NASV

The Will to Love

**"Lord, accept our willingness
and forgive our weakness."**

Spurgeon

"Lord, I am not willing!"
"Are you willing to be made willing?"

Rees Howels

*T*he floodgate of loving is the will. The reservoir of our heart may be overflowing with good intentions to love, but the life-giving flow to others is dependent upon a decision of the will. Often we wait for the feeling of love. When we will to do and say what love demands, we will have the power for what love requires. We can ask, "If I loved God with all my heart, what would I do?" Get that clearly portrayed in the imagination. Then will to do it.

Jesus focused a good deal of His ministry on the will. He knew that the convictions of the mind and the emotions of the heart require obedience of the will. The surrender of the will to Him provides Him with a ready instrument with which He can love. He asks us what He asked Rees Howels, "Are you willing to be made willing?"

"If any man is willing to do His will, he shall know...."

John 7:17, NASV

"Nevertheless, not my will but Thine be done."

Luke 22:42

Love for Ourselves

There is no more frustrating challenge than to be told to love ourselves. How can we?

*W*e know what we are—really. All the hidden memories known only to us mock any love for ourselves. How can we love the person inside us, knowing all we've said and done? Add to that all the negative impact of others who are often so starved for love themselves that they can do little but reinforce our self-depreciation.

A lively self-esteem is a rare gift. That's why only Christ's love can break the bind of self-negation and justification. When we accept His unqualified love, we can dare to love the person He loves so much. It is a psychological law, as irrevocable as a natural law of gravity, that we can't love anyone else until we are freed to love ourselves. A new freedom to be loving begins in a healing experience of Christ's love, acceptance and forgiveness.

"You shall love
your neighbor as yourself."
Matthew 22:39, NKJB

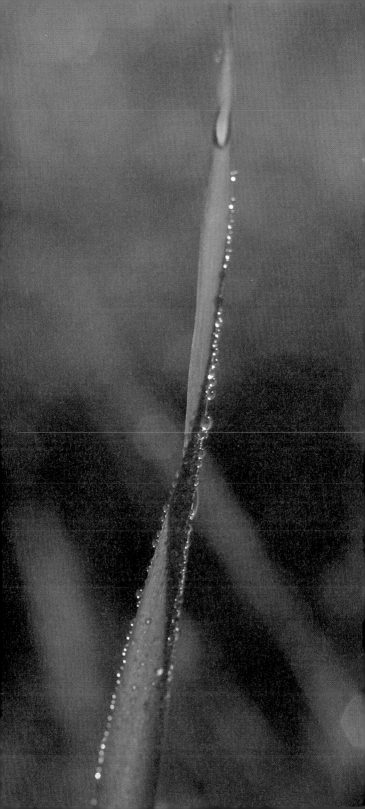

"Immortal Love, forever full,
Forever flowing free,
Forever shared, forever whole
A never-ebbing sea."

Whittier

Say It!

I was startled by a poster. The words were meant to be humorous, but they had a haunting residual. "Do you love me or do you not? You told me once, but I forgot."

Verbal expressions of love are healing, liberating. Why is it that it's so difficult to assure our loved ones and friends how much we love them? A Vermont farmer with laconic reserve said to his wife, "Martha, I love you so much, it's almost more than I can do not to tell you!" We laugh at that but then begin to wonder who in our life needs to have the dry places in their hearts watered by words of love.

Shakespeare said, "They do not love, that do not show their love." Words do not substitute for action, nor action for words. The most powerful words ever spoken are, "I love you!"

"We are bound to thank God always for you, brethren, as it is fitting, because your faith grows exceedingly, and the love of every one of you all abounds toward each other...."

II Thessalonians 1:3, NKJB

Love in the Perfect Tense

"Love is the perfect tense of the verb 'live.' Oh, to be intense in that perfect tense!"

Spurgeon

*T*he perfect tense expresses the continuance of completed action. Our love is the continuance of our Lord's completed love. His life in us is the secret source of our loving. He promised the abundant life to His followers. The abundance is more of Him!

The more we experience Christ, the more we will know of life as He meant it to be. When we find it difficult to love, the answer is not to condemn ourselves or search for some hidden psychological cause. Rather, it's a time for prayer. In the quiet we can open our need to Christ, tell Him our inadequacy and impotence to love profoundly. The amazing delight will be a new power flowing into us beyond our capacity. Inadvertently, a fresh flow of love for people will surprise us— and the people we long to love.

"I came that they might have life and might have it abundantly."

John 10:10, ASV

Allow God to Love You!

When we allow God to love us, we can open all the hidden resources of our personality to Him. He knows all about us, anyway. Real love replaces self-generated efforts of adequacy with intimacy. That means opening our innermost being so that our intrinsic self may be known in a profound, personal friendship with the Lord.

He has shown us His essential nature in the incarnation. We have been given the freedom to remain open or closed to Him. Though He knows all about our innermost thoughts, He will not invade our privacy without our invitation. But He will persist until we say, "Lord, You know all about me and love me just as I am, in spite of everything. Now I want You to not only love me but make me the lover of others You intended." Life really begins when we allow God to love us. The abundant life is not straining to love God, but opening ourselves to His love. Then we will love because we are loved. What a difference!

"We love, because He first loved us."
I John 4:19, NASV

"Do you love me? Feed My sheep."

John 21:17, RSV

Do You Love Me?

Suddenly it was quiet around the fire beside the Sea of Galilee. The other disciples had drifted away after breakfast. Only the resurrected Lord and Peter remained.

Peter could not lift his eyes. His heart ached with the anguish of his denial. Jesus broke the silence. "Simon, son of John, do you love Me more than these?" The fishing nets, his friends and old life.

The words cut like a knife. Peter had said he loved the Lord and would never deny Him. Christ used Peter's own words.

Peter replied, "Yes, Lord, You know I am Your friend." The Lord had asked about love and Peter, now humiliated by his failure, replied with the word for friend. He could be sure of that.

The Lord asked the question three times, once for each of the three denials. Each time Peter protested his friendship. Finally the Lord said, "Are you really My friend? Then, feed My sheep."

The sure sign that we love Christ is that we love others with the power of His love. He comes to each of us with the chance of a new beginning. If we love Him, we will long to love as we've been loved.

New Every Morning

As the Lord gives the day, He shows the way. He never gives us more to face in any one day than the knowledge and experience of His steadfast love will sustain.

*W*hen we begin each day with conversation with our Lord, He assures us of His never-ceasing love. Our emptiness is filled by His own Spirit of love. Each day it is new, fresh, energizing. We can start out on the adventure of each day with "I am loved, yesterday is past, tomorrow is in His care, and I can live to the hilt today." Often the reason we find it difficult to love others is that we have not had a daily reaffirmation of God's faithful love. Today can be the most exciting day of our lives.

"But this I call to mind, and therefore I have hope: The steadfast love of the Lord never ceases, His mercies never come to an end; they are new every morning; great is Thy faithfulness."

Lamentations 3:21-23, RSV

Now, Now, Now!

"Love them now, not after they've gone away."   Avery and Marsh

"The future has a habit of suddenly and dramatically becoming the present."   Roger Babson

"I expect to spend the rest of my life in the future, so I want to be reasonably sure of the kind of future it's going to be."   Charles Kettering

Now! What an exciting word. Our future is the result of what we do with the present. Now is all we have. Love to the hilt in the present, and the future will be beyond our fondest dreams.

The temptation to put loving off to some magic moment in the future is to miss the opportunity which will never return in the same way. Life slips by quickly, and we are left with the "what ifs" and "what might have beens" of life. The present now is what we give to God; the future is what He gives us in return.

"Behold, now is the acceptable time; Behold, now is the day of salvation."
      II Corinthians 6:2, NASV

"Make the most of every opportunity."
      Colossians 4:5, NIV

"So teach us to number our days that we may get to the heart of wisdom."

Psalm 90:12, TLB

"Look carefully how you walk, not as unwise men but as wise, making the most of the time."

Ephesians 5:15-16, RSV

Love Takes Time

"If I cannot give my children a perfect mother, I can at least give them more of the one they've got—and make that one more loving. I will be available. I will take time to listen, time to play, time to be home when they arrive from school, time to counsel and encourage."

Ruth Bell Graham

One of the most crucial discoveries I've made about love is that it takes time. I don't mean that it takes a long time to grow, but it requires time in which to be expressed. Unplanned and unstructured time with our family and friends strengthens the bond of love. In our personal lives, the gift of leisurely time to enjoy another person is an expression of love. It is then that we can listen, share deepest feelings, exchange hopes and unwrap the unique gift God gives us in a person. God always has all the time in the world for us.

"For everything there is a season, and a time for every matter under heaven."

Ecclesiastes 3:1, RSV

"Love is the greatest thing God can give us; for Himself is love: and it is the greatest thing we can give to God."

Jeremy Taylor

What Is Love?

Whatis this many-splendored thing we call love? We talk about it and sing ballads to express it. We can with the same breath say, "I love that place!" and "I love you!" and mean something very different. To some, love means a feeling, to others a conviction, to still others a loyalty.

Love is the one capacity which is experienced and expressed by every facet of our being. It is mental, emotional, volitional and physical. The reason is that we were created for love and to love. God is love. He created us to be recipients of His love and be lovers of others. The sublime fulfillment of our destiny is to receive His love and love people as He has loved us. God's love revealed in Christ is free, giving, forgiving and totally unconditioned by what we do or say. The love-shaped vacuum in all of us is God's gift. It makes us capable of believing, knowing, feeling that we are loved by Him.

"And we have known and believed the love that God has for us. God is love, and he who dwells in love dwells in God, and God in him."

I John 4:16, NKJB

Loving Impossible People

"Whoso loves believes the impossible."

Elizabeth Barrett Browning

A woman shared her ambivalent heart. "I love him but I don't like him!" Can we love without liking? Isn't liking love in expression? We would all empathize with the woman. There are people we dislike because of what they do and say.

What can we do with our negative feelings about certain people? How can we overcome our critical judgments which block the flow of love? People desperately need to be liked as part of our loving. They need to know that we are delighted in them.

The only way that I've ever conquered my dislikes is by daring to care. Distressing people drive us to our knees, pleading for the power to love profoundly enough to be able to help a person with the things which distress us.

It is in prayer that the Lord allows us to see ourselves and all He has endured in us. Then He helps us to truly see the persons we dislike in their need and what has made them what they are. Then He says, "This task is too big for you alone. Let Me love them through you. Trust Me. I will surprise you with the power to love and like, and you will be amazed that these people will begin to change the very things which distressed you." Nothing is impossible when we trust God—not even impossible people!

"If you can believe, all things are possible to him who believes."

Mark 9:23, NKJB

Love Casts Out Fear

"God Incarnate is the end of fear; and the heart that realizes that He is in the midst, that takes heed to the assurance of His loving presence, will be quiet in the midst of alarm."

F. B. Meyer

What makes you afraid? We begin life with fear of loud noises. As we grow, we fear darkness or falling. By the time we are adolescents, our emotional circuits are loaded with conditioned fears ingrained by parents and friends. The contagion of fear is epidemic in our society. We fear failure, certain kinds of people, the unexpected and the untried.

Fear, not just hate, is the opposite of love. The same emotional channels which carry the heavy freight of fear were meant to receive and express the liberating power of love. Surrender to our Lord what makes you afraid. Then, picture Him with you in the situation or relationship you fear. Listen to what He said to the disciples on the storming sea, "I am, do not be afraid." Disown the fear; displace it with His love!

"There is no fear in love, but perfect love casts out fear. For fear has to do with punishment, and he who fears is not perfected in love."

I John 4:18, RSV

No Longer an Enemy

**"He who has a thousand friends has not a friend to spare,
And he who has one enemy will meet him everywhere."**

*W*hat if we are our own worst enemy? When we get down on ourselves, we are soon negative and hostile to others. We find fault, criticize and become suspicious. People become our enemies, but the real enemy is inside ourselves.

John Ruskin said, "When a man is all wrapped up in himself, he makes a pretty small package." We become little packages of self-centered anger until God invades our hearts with amazing grace.

The most startling result of a profound experience of love is that we begin to see people differently. No longer threatening enemies, they are the lonely in need of our love, the afraid in need of our assurance, the insecure in need of our affirmation.

"For if when we were enemies we were reconciled to God by the death of His Son, much more, having been reconciled, we shall be saved by His life."

Romans 5:10, NKJB

Contagious Love

"When iron is rubbed against a magnet it becomes magnetic. Just so, love is caught, not taught. Our heart burning with love sets another on fire."

Frank Laubach

One of the finest things I have ever heard said about a person is, "He has the fires of God's love burning inside him. You can't be with him for very long until you feel the icy fingers of fear and doubt melt from around your own heart."

The man is one of my best friends. The fire of the Holy Spirit burns in him. He has a gracious warmth that communicates acceptance and confidence to others. The remarkable thing is that, a few years ago, he was a hostile, negative pharisee. He believed in Christ but had not allowed His Spirit to heal him with love.

A painful tragedy in his family forced him to see how little emotional warmth had been communicated by him. He asked for the Lord's forgiveness and for the infilling of His Spirit. The dry kindling of his heart was set ablaze. You cannot be with him without the flames leaping from his heart to yours.

"Do not quench the Spirit."
I Thessalonians 5:19, NKJB

The Gift of Love

All efforts to define love fall dumb before the Apostle Paul's magnificent hymn of love in I Corinthians, chapter 13.

*J*t is a description of Christ and the love He enables in us when He comes to indwell us.

The passage comes alive when it is read three ways. First, read it as Paul wrote it; next, put the word Christ in place of the word love and read it again; then, replace the word love with the personal pronoun "I" and read it once more. The miracle of Christ's indwelling power is that the love He revealed is exactly the love He will communicate to others through us.

If I had the gift of being able to speak in other languages without learning them, and could speak in every language there is in all of heaven and earth, but didn't love others, I would only be making noise. If I had the gift of prophecy and knew all about what is going to happen in the future, knew everything about everything, but didn't love others, what good would it do? Even if I had the gift of faith so that I could speak to a mountain and make it move, I would still be worth nothing at all without love. If I gave everything I have to poor people, and if I were burned alive for preaching the Gospel but didn't love others, it would be of no value whatever.

Love is very patient and kind, never jealous or envious, never boastful or proud, never haughty or selfish or rude. Love does not demand its own way. It is not irritable or touchy. It does not hold grudges and will hardly even notice when others do it wrong. It is never glad about injustice, but rejoices whenever truth wins out.

If you love someone you will be loyal to him no matter what the cost. You will always believe in him, always expect the best of him, and always stand your ground in defending him. All the special gifts and powers from God will someday come to an end, but love goes on forever."

I Corinthians 13:1-8, TLB

Ring the Bell!

"He who loves not, lives not."

Ramon Lull

Mary Martin was facing a difficult time physically and emotionally. She needed courage and fortitude. One night, at curtain-time, she was not sure that she could go on stage for one more performance.

There was a knock at her dressing room door. A messenger handed her a note. It was from her friend Oscar Hammerstein. It communicated love and encouragement and included these words: "A bell is a bell if you ring it, and love is love when you give it."

Miss Martin went on stage to give one of her finest performances. She gave herself away. She never forgot the challenge to ring the bell! Love is entrusted to us by God to give away.

"And let us not grow weary while doing good, for in due season we shall reap if we do not lose heart. Therefore, as we have opportunity, let us do good to all...."

Galatians 6:9-10, NKJB

Love Is Its Own Reward

"Love seeks one thing only: the good of the one loved. It leaves all other secondary effects to take care of themselves. Love, therefore, is its own reward."

Thomas Merton

What does it mean to love?

To love is to will the ultimate good of another. The key is the word ultimate. When we love God with all our minds and hearts and ask Him to guide us in our loving, He will reveal the best among the good alternatives. There are times that love requires firmness and honesty, directness and decisiveness.

Temporary pain is better than an easy way that leads to ruin. If we discern the word or action that will enable a person to grow and experience full potential, the Lord will take care of the rest. Love without honesty is sentimentality; honesty without love is severity. The Lord wills and enables an ultimate good and trains us in loving others as He has loved us.

"Let love be genuine; hate what is evil, hold fast to what is good, love one another with brotherly affection."

Romans 12:9-10, RSV

"I have been crucified with Christ; it is no longer I who live, but Christ lives in me."

Galatians 2:20, NKJB

"We know that we have passed from death to life, because we love...."

I John 3:14, NKJB

A.D. Love

"One way of putting the question to ourselves is: are we being B.C. or A.D.? Are the standards of greatness which you accept those that for the most part pervaded before Christ came into the world with His insistence on a new measurement of service, or are you living in some year of our Lord?"

Helford Luccock

A.D. love is empowered by the Lord Himself. It is vibrant with post-resurrection resiliency. Love before Christ was measured, qualified, limited. Christ called His disciples to love one another, people of all nations and their enemies. His love combines words and action. The cross revealed the extent of His love, and the resurrection displayed its unconquerable power.

But Christ has given us more than a message and mandate about love. He gives Himself. A.D. love is allowing Him to motivate and mediate His own love through us. The dynamic of Christianity is dying to ourselves and being raised to be filled with the Lord and His Spirit of love.

The Power Connection

"I am to become a Christ to my neighbor and be for him what Christ is for me."

Martin Luther

*J*esus' admonition to love is impossible without a constant flow of His Spirit into us. We cannot give away what we have not received.

The Lord gave us the secret in the powerful image of the vine and the branches. A branch separated from the vine is cut off from the life-giving sap. The Lord's warning is, "Apart from Me you can do nothing." We cannot love without His love moving from the vine into the branches.

The power connection is absolutely necessary. We are not called to attempt to love for His glory. Rather, we are to develop a moment-by-moment dependence upon His Spirit flowing into us and through us to people. Root and fruit are inseparably related.

"I am the vine, you are the branches. He who abides in Me and I in him, bears much fruit; for without Me you can do nothing."
"This is my commandment, that you love one another as I have loved you."

John 15:5, 12, NKJB

Love Bids Us Go!

"Tell me how much you know of the sufferings of your fellow men and I will tell you how much you have loved them."

Helmut Thielicke

In times of suffering we ask, "How can I get out of this?" Our temptation is to think that we are alone, that no one else has ever gone through what we are going through.

What we need is a caring, sharing love. Love chooses to become involved. We need interpretation and inspiration. Someone who loves us will lift the burden by telling us what he or she discovered in suffering and what was learned in the tight places. We do not need glib phrases but truth tempered in the fires of experience.

Who in our circle of influence are suffering? Love bids us to go to them. Everything we have gone through is equipment for identifying love. Then we can share the strength the Lord provides in suffering.

"By this we know love, because He laid down His life for us. And we ought to lay down our lives for the brethren."

I John 3:16, NKJB

Love
Without Limits

"He giveth more grace as the burdens
   grow greater,
He sendeth more strength as the labors
   increase.
To added affliction, He addeth His
   mercy,
To multiplied trials His multiplied
   peace.
When we have exhausted our store of
   endurance,
When our strength has failed ere the
   day is half done,
When we reach the end of our hoarded
   resources,
Our Father's full giving is only begun.
His love has no limits, His grace has no
   measure,
His power no boundary known to men.
And out of His infinite riches in Jesus,
He giveth, and giveth, and giveth
   again."
                                    Annie Johnson Flint

The beauty of love comes from the
limitless eternal springs of God's
heart. He created us out of love, for
love, and to love. It is the reason we
were born. Life really begins when we
receive unlimited love and dare to
love without limits.

" 'I can forgive, but I can't forget' is only another way of saying, 'I will not forgive.' "

Henry Ward Beecher

Love and Forgiveness

"To err is human, to forgive divine."

Alexander Pope

Eventually, every relationship is tested by the necessity to forgive. When we say we forgive but brood over the memory of the hurt or failure, we have not forgiven. The Lord's forgiveness is so complete that He relates to us as if we had never sinned. That's the awesome message of the cross. "Father, forgive them" is the constant, eternal expression of love that forgives even before we ask.

Arthur's magnanimous word to Guinevere in *The Idylls of the King* portrays the depth of true love and forgiveness: "And all is past, the sin is sinned, and lo, I forgive thee as Eternal God forgives." Love and forgiveness are inseparable.

"Forgive us our sins, just as we have forgiven those who have sinned against us."

Matthew 6:12, TLB

"Be kind to one another, tenderhearted, forgiving one another as God in Christ forgave you."

Ephesians 4:32, RSV

When Love Is Blocked

"Everything can be taken from us but one thing—the last of the human freedoms—to choose one's attitude in any given circumstance."

Victor Frankl

"*I* just don't love Him anymore. Something has happened; I don't feel the way I did. Is it possible to fall out of love?" The woman's earnest question explained her broken relationship with her husband.

The same question could be asked about friends. Have you ever experienced a time when your love for a person has grown dull and dim? Often, it's not just what a person has done but our lack of honesty about our feelings. We think of ourselves as magnanimous people who are all-accepting. Yet the actions of others distress us.

No one thing destroys a love relationship. Little things pile up. Soon our feelings are blocked. Then it's time to talk to God and eventually to the person. God will give us the graciousness to share our frustrations and misunderstandings in a way that will not make the person defensive. People don't fall out of love; they hide their hurts. God wants to free the channel if we are willing. God's love for us enables us to make our needs known in a way that others can respond to creatively.

The Bread of Life

"A thankful heart is not only the greatest virtue, but the parent of all other virtues."

Cicero

"Every virtue divorced from thankfulness is maimed and limps along the spiritual road."

John Henry Jowett

"A Christian is one who never forgets for a moment what God has done for him in Christ."

John Baillie

We are dependent upon God for everything. We could not breathe a breath, think a thought, move a muscle, work a day, or develop our lives without His moment-by-moment provision. Put your finger on your pulse; thank God for your life. Breathe in, saying, "Bless the Lord, O my soul"; breathe out, saying, "And all that is within me, bless His holy name."

List what is yours from God's loving provision. Praise Him for food, your body, the people of your life, the opportunities and the challenges of today. Daily bread is more than food to eat. Through the Bread of Life, Jesus Christ, all things we have and are become an evidence of unmerited favor from a Lord who knows our needs. Make this a day for "flash prayers" in which you repeatedly say, "Thank You, Lord," for the abundant mercies in every moment of life.

"Bless the Lord, O my soul; and all that is within me, bless His holy name! Bless the Lord, O my soul, and forget not all His benefits."

Psalm 103:1-2, RSV

The Cross in the Heart of God

**I sometimes think about the Cross
and shut my eyes to try to see
The cruel nails and crown of thorns
and Jesus crucified for me.
But even could I see Him die,
I could not see a little part
Of that great love which, like a fire,
Is always burning in His heart.**

There was a cross in the heart of God before there was a cross on Golgotha. The love of God is the same yesterday, today and tomorrow. When we experience the cross, we know how much He loves us. The cross was then and is now; if it was only then and not now, we've missed the pulsebeat of His relentless grace.

"And we have come to know and have believed the love which God has for us. God is love, and the one who abides in love abides in God, and God abides in him."

I John 4:16, ASV

The Limitless Source

"Have this attitude in yourselves which was also in Christ Jesus."

Philippians 2:5, ASV

*T*o have the mind of Christ is to have His attitude and disposition. The word for "mind" in Greek also means attitude and disposition. When we reflect upon His attitudes and His consistent disposition toward others, we begin to catch the vision of what He wants to manifest through us.

A new creature in Christ is one who can love, forgive, care and empathize with His indwelling Spirit as the motivating, engendering power. The Christian life is life as Christ lived it, life as we live it in Him, and life as He lives it through us. Our task is to be a channel, not a reservoir. Inflow and outflow of love are perfectly measured.

"For who has known the mind of the Lord, that he should instruct Him?
But we have the mind of Christ."

I Corinthians 2:16, ASV

A Prayer to
Be a Miracle

Living Lord Jesus,
I want to know You and
Your unqualified love.
Thank You for dying for me.
Your love for me right now
melts the cold resistance of my heart.
By faith I accept Your forgiveness
for the sin of running my own life
and limiting the immense possibilities
of the love You offer
to communicate through me.
I want to know You
and experience life
through the power of Your Spirit.
I surrender myself
and all my relationships to You.

Here is my mind,
think through it to show me
what love demands;
here is my will,
guide and direct all my words and
    actions;
here is my heart,
come and live in me to make me warm,
affirming and accepting.
Make me a miracle of love now.
I want to be to others
what You have been to me.
Thank You, Lord,
that, with this commitment,
I have died to myself
and am alive forever.
All things are possible now.

Hallelujah and Amen.

GIFT BOOKS FOR ALL OCCASIONS BY
LLOYD JOHN OGILVIE

- *BEAUTY OF CARING*
- *BEAUTY OF SHARING*
- *BEAUTY OF FRIENDSHIP*
- *BEAUTY OF LOVE*

OTHER BOOKS BY
LLOYD JOHN OGILVIE:

- *GOD'S BEST FOR MY LIFE (A day-by-day
  devotional)*
- *DISCOVERING GOD'S WILL IN YOUR
  LIFE*
- *FREEDOM IN THE SPIRIT*

Available at your local bookstore or:

Harvest House Publishers
1075 Arrowsmith
Eugene, OR 97402

Photo Credits:

Dale Beers; pages 6, 17, 23

Scoti Domeij; pages 51, 58, 61

William Jensen; pages 49, 52

All other photos by
Koechel/Peterson Design